**Purpose to Overcome**

Purpose to Overcome Through Prayer

A 30 Day Devotional

 **Purpose to Overcome**

Contents

Introduction	**4**
How to use this book	**6**
Day 01 to Day 30	**10**
Testimonials	**73**
What next?	**77**

Purpose to Overcome

 Purpose to Overcome

Introduction

Sometimes, you sense a need for change, a stirring in your heart, a whisper from God calling you to rise above where you are.

You desire more in your Christian life to overcome the obstacles that hinder your faith. You want to hear from God with greater clarity, and cultivate a deeper, unshakable relationship with Him.

Prayer is the key

Nothing in this world can replace the power of one-on-one conversation with the Almighty Creator, our friend, Savior, and guide.

A group of women made a commitment to pursue that deeper relationship. Together, they sought not only to grow closer to God but to overcome the challenges, doubts, and distractions that threatened their walk with Him.

Through scripture, prayer, and reflection, they experienced breakthroughs that transformed their spiritual lives.

This book is a collection of the scriptures and reflections that guided them day after day to overcome. It is designed to help you, find strength and clarity as you overcome life's hurdles and draw closer to God

 Purpose to Overcome

Our prayer is that as you embark on this 30-day journey, you will experience what they did: peace, purpose, and a renewed connection with Christ Jesus. He is the one who enables us to overcome all things.

Special recognition goes to:

Our Pastor Louis Farquharson for his insight and teaching on the topic 'Purpose to Overcome'.

Also, the following women for their commitment to daily prayer and the help to prepare this devotional so that others can grow in prayer:

Anya Anderson, Amanda Anderson, Verona Black, Laverne Baptiste, Cleoverne Baptiste, Frances Farquharson, Melissa Farquharson, Beryl Nyerere, Alice Nahimana & Sandra Smith.

God bless you.

Denise Farquharson

King's Chapel Apostolic Church, Ladies Leader.

 **Purpose to Overcome**

How to Use This 30-Day Prayer Devotional

This devotional is designed to deepen your connection with God and help you grow spiritually over the next 30 days. Follow these steps to get the most out of each day's scripture, reflection, and prayer:

1. Prepare Your Heart and Mind

- **Find a Quiet Space**: Set aside a specific time and place each day where you can focus without distractions.

- **Pray Before You Begin**: Ask God to open your heart, guide your understanding, and reveal His message for you in the scripture.

2. Read the Scripture with Intention

- **Read Slowly**: Take time to carefully read the scripture for the day, paying attention to words or phrases that stand out.

- **Read Again, if Needed**: Meditate on the passage, allowing the meaning to sink in.

 Purpose to Overcome

3. Reflect on What You've Read

- **Ask Questions**:
    - What is God revealing to me through this scripture?
    - How does this passage connect to my current situation or struggles?
- **Write It Down**: Use the space to document your thoughts, emotions, reflections or any revelations you've received.

---

4. Apply the Scripture to Your Life

- **Personal Application**: Consider how you can put the message into practice in your daily life.
    - Does it challenge you to change a habit or attitude?
    - Does it encourage you to take action to overcome, or offer forgiveness?
- **Share with Someone**: Discuss the scripture with someone else to gain deeper insights or encourage others.

Purpose to Overcome

5. Test and Practice the Recommendations

- **Act on the Principles**: If the devotional offers practical steps or recommendations, try them out in your daily routine.
    - For example, if the passage calls for a change of mind, make a conscious effort to practice it throughout the day.
- **Evaluate Your Growth**: At the end of the day or week, ask yourself:
    - Have I noticed changes in my thoughts, actions, or relationships?
    - Am I living as an overcomer and more closely aligned with God's Word?

 **Purpose to Overcome**

6. Review and Revisit

- **Go Back to Key Passages**: If a particular day's scripture deeply resonated with you, revisit it to reinforce its impact.

- **Pray Over Your Progress**: Reflect on what God has been teaching you throughout the devotional and seek His guidance for continued growth.

- **Celebrate Your Journey**: Recognize the spiritual progress you've made and thank God for His faithfulness.

Final Thoughts

This devotional is more than a daily routine; it's an opportunity to draw closer to God, align your life with His Word, and discover His purpose for you. Approach each day with expectation, humility, and a willingness to overcome.

Purpose to Overcome

Day 01

Scripture

Numbers 13: 30

And Caleb stilled the people before Moses, and said, let us go up at once, and possess it; for we are well able to overcome it.

Reflections from Scripture

Sometimes you need to open your mouth and declare the impossible.

That's how hope is created, and your belief level gets stronger.

Caleb was more than just being optimistic; his faith level became strong.

Why not be strong and of good courage?

Pray like Caleb today and don't be dismayed.

 **Purpose to Overcome**

Write your own reflections, prayer and testimonies here…

Purpose to Overcome

Day 02

Scripture

Revelation 3: 12

Him that overcometh will I make a pillar in the temple of my God, and he shall go no more out: and I will write upon him the name of my God, and the name of the city of my God, which is new Jerusalem, which cometh down out of heaven from my God: and I will write upon him my new name.

Reflections from Scripture

Let your heart burn with passion and purpose, refusing to be lukewarm in your walk with Him. Embrace a life of surrender, breaking free from every stronghold that seeks to bind you.

Embrace a life that overcomes.

Trust in His power to renew relationships and open unexpected doors of opportunity. See walls not as barriers but as invitations for breakthrough—push forward in faith!

Declare boldly: this day, this week, this month, this year, is mine.

It's a season of victory and transformation!

Purpose to Overcome

Write your own reflections, prayer and testimonies here…

Purpose to Overcome

Day 03

Scripture

Proverbs 3: 5 -6

v5: Trust in the LORD with all thine heart; and lean not unto thine own understanding.

V6: In all thy ways acknowledge him, and he shall direct thy paths.

Reflections from Scripture

To begin overcoming any situation, you must first trust God with everything—fully and completely.

Today, as you pray, ask Him to open your heart and reveal what lies within. When He shows you, reflect on it:

Does it allow you to truly trust Him? If the answer is no, bring it to Him in prayer. Ask for the strength and faith to release it into His hands.

What's holding back your trust may be the very thing He wants to transform, and as you pray it through, you'll step into a more powerful walk with Him.

Purpose to Overcome

Write your own reflections, prayer and testimonies here…

Purpose to Overcome

Day 04

Scripture

1 John 5: v1 and v4

v1: Whosoever believeth that Jesus is the Christ is born of God: and every one that loveth him that begat loveth him also that is begotten of him.

v4: For whatsoever is born of God overcometh the world: and this is the victory that overcometh the world, even our faith.

Reflections from Scripture

Here is a simple prayer for you. Adapt it to suit your situation.

"Grant me the strength, O Lord, to stand firm against the evils that seek to sway my heart. Help me to nurture relationships with love and grace, healing what is broken and building what is good.

Guide me to overcome desires, both emotional and physical, that lead me away from Your path.

Transform my habits, shaping them to reflect Your will, so I'll grow in discipline and righteousness. May Your strength flow through me, renewing my spirit each day- Amen."

 **Purpose to Overcome**

Write your own reflections, prayer and testimonies here…

Purpose to Overcome

Day 05

Scripture

Romans 12:2

And be not conformed to this world: but be ye transformed by the renewing of your mind, that ye may prove what *is* that good, and acceptable, and perfect, will of God.

Reflections from Scripture

Overcomers only conform to things that create a spirit of resolve and determination inside of them.

Overcomers transform their mind because it can be a battlefield.

Set it straight through daily prayer, talking to the Lord and spending quality time exploring the Word at a deeper level.

When you do that, you will see the impact and the changes in your spiritual walk with Christ.

Purpose to Overcome

Write your own reflections, prayer and testimonies here…

Purpose to Overcome

Day 06

Scripture

Matthew 5: 10 – 12

v10: Blessed *are* they which are persecuted for righteousness' sake: for theirs is the kingdom of heaven.
v11: Blessed are ye, when *men* shall revile you, and persecute *you,* and shall say all manner of evil against you falsely, for my sake.
v12: Rejoice and be exceeding glad: for great *is* your reward in heaven: for so persecuted they the prophets which were before you.

Reflections from Scripture

These verses beautifully illustrate the character we are called to cultivate in Christ. Grow in them you to open yourself to greater blessings. As those blessings fill your life, you'll overcome sin, shift unhealthy mindsets, and face life's challenges with strength and grace.

Take a moment today to practice humility, show compassion, and let your light shine brightly. Encourage others to also shine and stand firm in their faith and convictions.

Remember, prayer uproots pride, fasting breaks the grip of lust, and generosity frees you from the chains of greed. Together, these practices lead to a transformed, victorious life in Christ.

 **Purpose to Overcome**

Write your own reflections, prayer and testimonies here…

Purpose to Overcome

Day 07

Scripture

John 14:26 – 27

v26: But the Comforter, *which is* the Holy Ghost, whom the Father will send in my name, he shall teach you all things, and bring all things to your remembrance, whatsoever I have said unto you.

v27: Peace I leave with you, my peace I give unto you: not as the world giveth, give I unto you. Let not your heart be troubled, neither let it be afraid.

Reflections from Scripture

Christ will give his peace when you feel like you are not overcoming situations in your life. Here are some statements you can rely on to keep you on track.

He won't let your heart be troubled if you trust Him.

He is in you and you are in Him.

Prepare and be ready for Him to commune with you.

Go by faith, not by emotion and invest in your relationship with Him.

Prepare for the times when you are not able to pray.

 **Purpose to Overcome**

Write your own reflections, prayer and testimonies here…

Purpose to Overcome

Day 08

Scripture

Ephesians 6:10

Finally, my brethren, be strong in the Lord, and in the power of his might.

Reflections from Scripture

Roman soldiers often prepared and protected themselves with armour.

Today, why not focus on your armour to overcome:
- The shield of faith to overcome.
- The helmet of salvation to overcome.
- The sword of the Spirit to overcome.

These spiritual tools become your weapons to face life's battles with confidence. They remind you that victory is not by your strength alone, but through the power of God working in you.

As you put them on, you align yourself with His truth, His promises, and His unstoppable power.

It will make you strong, help you to walk right, and build that resolve inside of you.

Purpose to Overcome

Write your own reflections, prayer and testimonies here…

Purpose to Overcome

Day 09

Scripture

1 Chronicles 29: 11

Thine, O LORD, *is* the greatness, and the power, and the glory, and the victory, and the majesty: for all *that is* in the heaven and in the earth *is thine;* thine *is* the kingdom, O LORD, and thou art exalted as head above all.

Reflections from Scripture

Despite what you are going through today is the day to worship. Put aside any unimportant and non-urgent tasks and worship.

You can even use the bible verse and just worship Him. He loves when you worship and spend time with Him.

Worshipping takes your mind off the natural and focus on the supernatural presence of God to break down the chains and walls of life that may be restricting your spiritual freedom.

Worshippers are overcomers.

👑 Purpose to Overcome

Write your own reflections, prayer and testimonies here…

Purpose to Overcome

Day 10

Scripture

Jeremiah 29:13

And ye shall seek me, and find *me,* when ye shall search for me with all your heart.

Reflections from Scripture

Sometimes, we lose something in our home and no matter how hard we look, it feels impossible to find. But when we set aside focused time to search carefully, the joy we feel when it's found is immeasurable, and we can't wait to share the good news with others.

In the same way, when you seek Jesus earnestly in prayer, you will find Him—because He delights in being sought after by His children.

And when you encounter Him, you'll experience breakthroughs, freedom, and an overflow of love that impacts not only your life but the lives of those around you.

Purpose to Overcome

Write your own reflections, prayer and testimonies here…

Purpose to Overcome

Day 11

Scripture

Psalms 23 v 1-3

v1: The LORD *is* my shepherd; I shall not want.
v2: He maketh me to lie down in green pastures: he leadeth me beside the still waters.
v3: He restoreth my soul: he leadeth me in the paths of righteousness for his name's sake.

Reflections from Scripture

David understood the abundant blessings that come from God. As you read this Psalm, it becomes clear that he beautifully captures the attributes of the Great Shepherd—one who leads, protects, and provides.

Being with the Shepherd comes with incredible benefits, offering comfort and assurance no matter what you face.

Make a list of the things you need to overcome and bring them to God in prayer, one by one. Despite the current challenges you can have unshakable confidence.

The Great Shepherd is with you, and through Him, you can overcome.

Purpose to Overcome

Write your own reflections, prayer and testimonies here…

Purpose to Overcome

Day 12

Scripture

John 3:16

For God so loved the world, that he gave his only begotten Son, that whosoever believeth in him should not perish, but have everlasting life.

Reflections from Scripture

Because He loved, He gave.

Because He gave, we will not 'perish'

What an opportunity we have with such a loving God who was willing to sacrifice and provides a way for us to get through whatever struggles we face or issue we need to overcome.

Thank you, Lord!

He is a great example for us to follow.

So why not pray today, that you purpose to overcome any stubborn will, bad habits and any misguided thoughts.

You will be so glad that you did.

 **Purpose to Overcome**

Write your own reflections, prayer and testimonies here…

Purpose to Overcome

Day 13

Scripture

John 16:33

These things I have spoken unto you, that in me ye might have peace. In the world ye shall have tribulation: but be of good cheer; I have overcome the world.

Reflections from Scripture

We all want peace in our lives but what will it cost to have that peace? There are daily issues struggles and challenges that sometimes means we are not at peace.

But Jesus tells us to cheer up, be content, stay happy and be assured.

Why?

Simply because He has overcome the world.

So, despite how all these things make you feel, why don't you take time out today to pray and follow that commandment, be encouraged in yourself and take comfort in His words.

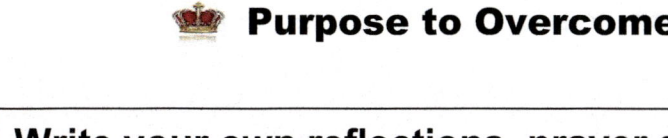 **Purpose to Overcome**

Write your own reflections, prayer and testimonies here…

Purpose to Overcome

Day 14

Scripture

Psalm 1 v 1

Blessed *is* the man that walketh not in the counsel of the ungodly, nor standeth in the way of sinners, nor sitteth in the seat of the scornful.

Reflections from Scripture

The counsel of the ungodly is simply not godly.

It will be packed with assumptions, sinful next steps and solutions that will not line up with Christ.

There is also a direct request not to be on the same journey and direction as sinners. Doing so does not help your purpose to overcome, neither does being in the presence of the scornful.

So, pray today to keep an eye on who you are listening to. Which direction are you going and where do you spend your time?

👑 Purpose to Overcome

Write your own reflections, prayer and testimonies here…

Purpose to Overcome

Day 15

Scripture

1 Peter 5: 7

Casting all your care upon him; for he careth for you.

Reflections from Scripture

When you throw something with force, it lands with impact—sometimes bouncing, breaking, flowing, or coming to a sudden stop. The same is true when you cast the cares of this world onto Him.

Something happens.

These cares—whether they are worries, doubts, pride, or lust—are burdens we were never meant to carry.

To overcome, we must release them fully, surrendering them to the One who is strong enough to bear them. Only then can we walk freely in His strength and peace.

Purpose to Overcome

Write your own reflections, prayer and testimonies here…

Purpose to Overcome

Day 16

Scripture

Isaiah 58:6

Is not this the fast that I have chosen? to loose the bands of wickedness, to undo the heavy burdens, and to let the oppressed go free, and that ye break every yoke?

Reflections from Scripture

When you genuinely want to overcome something, you may need to go into fasting. Fasting is good for the body, but it is also very good for the soul.

This verse describes four key things it can do for you.

Loose the bands of wickedness- e.g. lies, anger and shame.

Undo heavy burdens – violently agitate the challenges and issues to be no more.

Let the oppressed go free – exercise dominion over something.

Break every yoke – Christ is a yoke breaker of anything that hinders your spiritual growth.

Purpose to Overcome

Write your own reflections, prayer and testimonies here…

Purpose to Overcome

Day 17

Scripture

Jeremiah 29 v 11 to 13

v11: For I know the thoughts that I think toward you, saith the LORD, thoughts of peace, and not of evil, to give you an expected end.

v12: Then shall ye call upon me, and ye shall go and pray unto me, and I will hearken unto you.

v13: And ye shall seek me, and find *me,* when ye shall search for me with all your heart.

Reflections from Scripture

Thoughts that God thinks toward us is guaranteed to have an expected end. An outcome that brings benefits and joy to the believer.

But you must do something to make it come alive and that is to pray.

When you seek God in prayer with your heart, soul and mind, He will answer and His expected end WILL be seen in your life.

Purpose to Overcome

Write your own reflections, prayer and testimonies here…

Purpose to Overcome

Day 18

Scripture

Joel 2 v 23

Be glad then, ye children of Zion, and rejoice in the LORD your God: for he hath given you the former rain moderately, and he will cause to come down for you the rain, the former rain, and the latter rain in the first *month*.

Reflections from Scripture

Having God's rain poured down on you can be the most refreshing experiences. It can come in the form of the Holy Spirit's presence.

It creates soothing thoughts, peace of mind as well as powerful victorious praise and spiritual warfare.

When you pray today, ask God to pour that rain down on you. Create an overflow and abundance of favour and blessing.

Purpose to Overcome

Write your own reflections, prayer and testimonies here…

Purpose to Overcome

Day 19

Scripture

Psalms 121 v 1

I will lift up mine eyes unto the hills, from whence cometh my help.

Reflections from Scripture

When you say 'I will' it is a command to yourself that is certain, determined and resolute.

To overcome anything in your life you will have to move from a 'maybe' Christian talk to a determined 'I will' walk.

When you are intentional to look to God for help, He responds.

When you are purposed to make change God offers that help, and you start to see things change and make a difference in your life.

 **Purpose to Overcome**

Write your own reflections, prayer and testimonies here…

Purpose to Overcome

Day 20

Scripture

Psalms 8 v 6

Thou madest him to have dominion over the works of thy hands; thou hast put all *things* under his feet:

Reflections from Scripture

What an incredible privilege we hold as human beings in the hierarchy of God's kingdom. He created the earth for us, died on the cross for us, and left His Spirit to dwell within us.

Even the angels do not share these gifts, yet we, through the Spirit that raised Jesus from the dead, carry that same power within us. This is the power that enables us to overcome.

So, what challenges do you need to overcome in your family? Take it to God in prayer. Pray over your children, declare His presence in every room of your home, and release a spirit of freedom.

Set the spiritual thermostat of your home to "overcome" and invite His victory to reign in every corner of your life.

Purpose to Overcome

Write your own reflections, prayer and testimonies here…

Purpose to Overcome

Day 21

Scripture

1John 3: v 20 -22

v20: For if our heart condemn us, God is greater than our heart, and knoweth all things.

v21: Beloved, if our heart condemn us not, *then* have we confidence toward God.

v22: And whatsoever we ask, we receive of him, because we keep his commandments, and do those things that are pleasing in his sight.

Reflections from Scripture

What is motivating you to get up at this time in the morning to meet with God?

Ask yourself: - What is in my heart that I am still hiding and keeping buried?

Your heart can condemn you and it can keep you stuck in poor physical health conditions and affect your work relationships.

Every day during prayer ask God to cleanse your heart. Remove condemnation, not to give into shame and rise with a renewed mind.

Purpose to Overcome

Write your own reflections, prayer and testimonies here…

Purpose to Overcome

Day 22

Scripture

Luke 4: v1, v4, v14

v1: And Jesus being full of the Holy Ghost returned from Jordan, and was led by the Spirit into the wilderness,

v4: And Jesus answered him, saying, It is written, That man shall not live by bread alone, but by every word of God.

v14: And Jesus returned in the power of the Spirit into Galilee: and there went out a fame of him through all the region round about.

Reflections from Scripture

Jesus overcame temptation. That is a real consolation! Every Christian must go through temptation too, but we have the reassurance that He helps us overcome.

So, what is tempting you in your Christian journey and which temptation wins?

Christ showed us that it doesn't need to be a lot of warfare to win but it can simply be steps of discipline, humility and focus that will keep us on track.

Pray today about the temptations that come your way, so you can, through the strength of Christ overcome and win.

Purpose to Overcome

Write your own reflections, prayer and testimonies here…

Purpose to Overcome

Day 23

Scripture

Job 33:4

The Spirit of God hath made me, and the breath of the Almighty hath given me life

Reflections from Scripture

When we are struggling with life and feel we are on a losing battle, it can be hard. We may look to other things for solace, support and solutions.

But here God is telling us that he is your source because He has made you with His spirit. Therefore, we can be certain that He cares and will step in to help.

His breath has given us life so He will not just leave us to be wondering around trying to overcome all by ourselves. So why not simply trust His words, trust Him and watch what happens?

Purpose to Overcome

Write your own reflections, prayer and testimonies here…

Purpose to Overcome

Day 24

Scripture

Psalm 146:3

Put not your trust in princes, nor in the son of man, in whom there is no help.

Reflections from Scripture

What an interesting perspective coming from King David who wrote the Book of Psalm. He must have needed to depend on many others to rule his kingdom and those who lived in it.

I wonder if he experienced something with other people and had relationships where trust was built up but then destroyed.

If you need to overcome lust, guilt or shame, God wants you to trust Him and not anyone else to truly be transformed and renewed in your life.

Look at the relationships around you and make some decisions about how impactful or not they are on your path to overcoming.

Purpose to Overcome

Write your own reflections, prayer and testimonies here…

Purpose to Overcome

Day 25

Scripture

Genesis 19: 12 – 13

v12: And the men said unto Lot, Hast thou here any besides? son in law, and thy sons, and thy daughters, and whatsoever thou hast in the city, bring *them* out of this place:
v13: For we will destroy this place, because the cry of them is waxen great before the face of the LORD; and the LORD hath sent us to destroy it.

Reflections from Scripture

Lot was in a predicament. He made choices of where he would live, the exact location of his home, who would stay with him and who would be his friends.

We do the same thing and often do it without Gods help. But sometimes the decisions we make needs God right in the centre.

Deciding without him is a big risk and Lot unfortunately experienced the consequences of those choices.

So why not really listen carefully to what God is saying and purpose to do exactly what He says to do?

👑 Purpose to Overcome

Write your own reflections, prayer and testimonies here…

Purpose to Overcome

Day 26

Scripture

Psalms 27 v 1

The LORD *is* my light and my salvation; whom shall I fear? the LORD *is* the strength of my life; of whom shall I be afraid?

Reflections from Scripture

When we are in a state of feeling burdened, suppressed or weak, our life can feel down, and we may wonder if this is really what a Christian life is all about.

But Hallelujah! - His word confirms what He can offer.

Light – to see ahead more clearly.

Fearlessness – to step into a new way of living.

Strength – to carry your purpose for being here on earth.

Boldness - To step into a new spiritual path.

Go for it!

👑 Purpose to Overcome

Write your own reflections, prayer and testimonies here…

Purpose to Overcome

Day 27

Scripture

1 Peter 2:9

But ye *are* a chosen generation, a royal priesthood, an holy nation, a peculiar people; that ye should shew forth the praises of him who hath called you out of darkness into his marvellous light:

Reflections from Scripture

I love how God can pour out pure love, affirmations and uplifting words to His children. He means every word that He utters about you. Because of that we have a chance to grow in Christ in a way that supersedes any other relationship here on earth.

Pray that you accept that love He has for you.

Pray that you walk as a chosen one.

Pray with a heart of thanksgiving that He has called you out of bondage, chains, lust and a sinful life into His marvellous light.

Purpose to Overcome

Write your own reflections, prayer and testimonies here…

Purpose to Overcome

Day 28

Scripture

1 Corinthians 15: 57 – 58

v57: But thanks *be* to God, which giveth us the victory through our Lord Jesus Christ.

v58: Therefore, my beloved brethren, be ye steadfast, unmoveable, always abounding in the work of the Lord, forasmuch as ye know that your labour is not in vain in the Lord.

Reflections from Scripture

Take God's Word exactly as it is—His promises are true, and He does give you victory.

Living a victorious life means walking in His Word daily, learning, and growing in faith. Your victory isn't tied to your talents or skills but is made possible through the Lord Jesus. When He becomes the central focus of your life, everything else falls into place and flourishes.

So, keep pressing forward, stretching your faith, and reaching new heights in your journey with Him. Through His power, you will overcome every challenge and walk in victory without fail.

Purpose to Overcome

Write your own reflections, prayer and testimonies here…

Purpose to Overcome

Day 29

Scripture

Philippians 4: 6

Be careful for nothing; but in everything by prayer and supplication with thanksgiving let your requests be made known unto God.

Reflections from Scripture

Leaving things to chance is never wise. It opens the door to results and outcomes that may lead you away from your Christian journey.

Instead, be intentional and relentless in bringing everything to Jesus—your relationships, habits, patterns, and even the smallest things you notice in your walk with Him.

This command to bring everything to Him is not a burden but an invitation. It's an open door, assuring you that you'll never be bothering Him. Instead, you're granting Him full access to your every need, allowing Him to provide solutions to the challenges that stand in the way of your victory.

So today, let's pray and give Him everything.

Purpose to Overcome

Write your own reflections, prayer and testimonies here…

Purpose to Overcome

Day 30

Scripture

Psalms 150 v1, v2, v6

v1: Praise ye the LORD. Praise God in his sanctuary: praise him in the firmament of his power.

v2: Praise him for his mighty acts: praise him according to his excellent greatness.

v6: Let everything that hath breath praise the LORD. Praise ye the LORD.

Reflections from Scripture

An overcomer spends time praising God, rejoicing in every situation and gives thanks for every time a burden is lifted or there is a breakthrough in tricky circumstances.

Pray to always have a life of praise.

Pray to always praise even when you do not feel like it.

Pray to be wiser, humbler and more like our Lord every single day.

You're breathing - so praise away!

Purpose to Overcome

Write your own reflections, prayer and testimonies here…

Purpose to Overcome

Write your own reflections, prayer and testimonies here…

 **Purpose to Overcome**

Write your own reflections, prayer and testimonies here…

Purpose to Overcome

Write your own reflections, prayer and testimonies here…

 **Purpose to Overcome**

Testimonials

As you finish this journey, I encourage you to take the discipline of prayer and apply it to your own life. Feed the idea that prayer changes everything, nurture it daily, and watch how God works through you and those around you.

Testimonies are waiting to be written, and miracles are waiting to unfold through your commitment and God's unfailing power. Here are a few examples of it coming to life for the King's Chapel women who wanted to purpose to overcome.

~ Overcoming Finances! - One of the women in the group received a bill for over £600, demanding payment within a short period. She knew it was incorrect, as she had always kept her bills up to date. After praying together with a group of other ladies, she decided to challenge the bill. In response, the amount was significantly reduced to approximately £100 which was much more manageable.

~ Hallelujah Overcomers! - Another group member was actively searching for a new job closer to her home and family. This would significantly cut down her commute and offer better opportunities to grow her career. Prayers were made for her application, interview, and final decision to work in her favour, as well as for support and guidance on her first day at the new job.

Purpose to Overcome

~ That's God at work to overcome! - Being surrounded by family who don't believe in miracles or healing can be challenging. When the women decided to pray for a mother with a lump in her throat, they felt some anxiety and worry. But through dedicated prayer and consistent faith, the doctor later reviewed her condition and found nothing at all.

~ Thank God for young Christian overcomers! - A young member of the prayer group had a sincere desire to pray for their friends. They prayed with faith, and the answered prayers became powerful testimonies. One friend began asking more questions about Jesus, and another was healed from sickness. God has no age limit when it comes to answering prayers and helping you overcome.

~ Overcomers give thanks! - I spoke to one of the elderly ladies who has experienced God's healing power to overcome multiple sicknesses – This is what she said.

"God has done so much in my life and brought me out of sickness and so many other things. He's still keeping me and for that I give him thanks. So many prayers have gone up to the Almighty God from us ladies and we seem to have made a way and have answered prayers. There are so many more to answers to come."

 Purpose to Overcome

~ Stay consistent to overcome! - Being far from home can be tough and lonely, especially when your family is facing health challenges. One prayer member decided to focus deeply on prayer to overcome her family's illness. She prayed continuously for about two weeks, and then the good news started coming. Her family began to experience restored health, strength, and joy—beyond what was expected. Never underestimate the power of consistent prayer and supplication to the Lord.

~ God overcame so can you! - The eldest of the group had lost a loved one. It was a difficult journey filled with unexpected twists and turns. Losing a son before a parent passes away is especially heartbreaking. However, praying for someone in grief can bring incredible peace and comfort. They shared that even their tears no longer brought pain. Instead, sweet memories filled their mind, and they felt the warmth of the Holy Spirit in moments of emptiness.

~ Overcomers testify of the small and the great! - One of the ladies in our prayer group is always sharing testimonies of God's goodness and faithfully giving thanks to Him. She's thankful for His mercy and grace, and rightly so—God truly deserves it. Even when we forget whether a prayer has been answered, He is still worthy of our gratitude. In a world that often focuses on the struggles and unanswered questions, she inspires us to dwell instead on His countless blessings and steadfast love.

Purpose to Overcome

~ Lift your faith to overcome! - You've lost members of your family and the strain gets too much. One of the women has an ambulance rushed to their home with a suspected cardiac arrest. The women swept into action to pray with immediacy, focus and desperation. The paramedics find a left arial enlargement, but the doctors find nothing, the heart is beating as normal. This experience is a powerful reminder of the faithfulness of God and the power of prayer. In their darkest hour, these women leaned on their faith, trusting that God could do what seemed impossible. And He delivered.

~ Overcome sickness and be healed! - One woman decided to pray fervently for a friend who was facing the threat of blindness—and soon, light began to break through. She also prayed for another friend struggling with kidney issues, and within days, there was relief and a return to regular function. As she continued to lift her loved ones in prayer, breakthroughs came for her immediate family, freeing them from chains that had held them back for years. Her prayers became a powerful testament to God's ability to heal, restore, and deliver.

👑 Purpose to Overcome

What next?

If you used this devotional and want to explore how to get closer to God, here are three simple steps you can do to get started: - Scripture - Acts 2 v 37-38

Now when they heard this, they were pricked in their heart, and said unto Peter and to the rest of the apostles, Men and brethren, what shall we do?

Then Peter said unto them, Repent, and be baptized every one of you in the name of Jesus Christ for the remission of sins, and ye shall receive the gift of the Holy Ghost.

Repent – Let the Lord know you are sorry for your sins, and you want to take a different direction in your life. Ask God to forgive you, get rid of the things that cause you to sin and stay away from them.

Baptism – Seek a church that will baptise you for the remission of your sins in the name of the Lord Jesus Christ.

Holy Ghost – The spirit of Jesus Christ wants to live inside you. You can receive the Holy Spirit with the evidence of speaking in tongues through sincere prayer, faith in God's promise, and a willingness to fully surrender to His presence as He fills and empowers you.

References: All Scriptures taken from the King James Version of the Bible (KJV)
**Contact us - King's Apostolic Church, Coventry, UK.
Email: kings.chapel@ymail.com**

Printed in Great Britain
by Amazon